Cybersecurity Mistakes That Could Cost You Everything

How to Avoid the Costliest Security Errors Threatening Small Businesses Today

Written by
Eric LeBouthillier

AcraSolution | 2025 1st Edition
www.acrasolution.com

Preface

The truth is, most businesses aren't hacked by elite cybercriminals running dark-web operations.
They're breached by a missed update. A weak password. A team that doesn't know what a phishing link looks like.

And the worst part? The signs were there all along.

This book was written because I've seen the damage — data loss, financial collapse, reputations ruined — not from zero-day exploits or nation-state attacks, but from small, entirely preventable cybersecurity mistakes.

Whether you're running a business of one or leading a 20-person team, **you're a target** — not because of who you are, but because of what you have: access, customer data, systems, and a digital footprint.

Inside this book, I've laid out 15 of the most dangerous cybersecurity mistakes I've encountered — the kind that can cripple a company overnight — and more importantly, **exactly how to avoid them**.

This is not theory. It's battle-tested insight — stripped of fluff, built for action.

Let's fix what most overlook — before it costs you everything.

— *Eric LeBouthillier*
Author & Cybersecurity Strategist

Table of Contents

Who This Book Is For

This book is written for people who are responsible for security... but don't have "Cybersecurity" in their job title.

- Small and mid-sized business owners who want to avoid disaster without hiring a full-time security team
- Solopreneurs, freelancers, and consultants working with sensitive client data
- IT managers, developers, and operations leads building systems on a budget
- Founders scaling a startup and unsure where to start with security
- Digital agency owners and web professionals protecting customer platforms
- Anyone who believes "We're probably fine" — and wants to be sure

You don't need to be technical to read this book. You just need to be responsible for a system, a site, or a team that touches anything digital.

Because the biggest cybersecurity mistakes aren't about code. They're about **what we overlook, assume, or delay** — until it's too late.

Part I: Human Mistakes That Open the Door

Chapter 1: Thinking You're Too Small to Be a Target

Introduction

Too many small and mid-sized business (SMB) leaders still believe that cybersecurity threats are a big-business problem. After all, why would hackers bother with a 10-person accounting firm or a regional manufacturer when they could go after the giants? But the data tells a different story—one that could mean the difference between a thriving business and bankruptcy.

The truth is, cybercriminals *prefer* SMBs precisely because they assume they're not targets. These businesses often lack dedicated IT teams, have looser defenses, and can be compromised quickly. In today's threat landscape, assuming you're too small to be attacked is one of the costliest mistakes you can make.

This chapter breaks down that myth—and shows how even the smallest organization can put scalable, affordable defenses in place that drastically reduce risk.

Why SMBs Are Actually Prime Targets

Cyberattacks are a volume business. Most modern cybercrime is automated, meaning attackers use scripts and bots to scan the internet for vulnerabilities—not to seek out specific companies. These bots don't care how big your business is; they care whether your systems are exposed.

Key reasons SMBs are attractive to attackers:

- **Weaker defenses**: Many SMBs lack formal cybersecurity policies, tools, or training.
- **Faster payouts**: SMBs are more likely to pay ransoms quickly to recover operations.
- **Easy entry points**: Unpatched software, poor password habits, and legacy systems are common.
- **Gateway to larger networks**: SMBs in supply chains can be stepping stones to bigger enterprises.

Automated Bots Scanning the Web

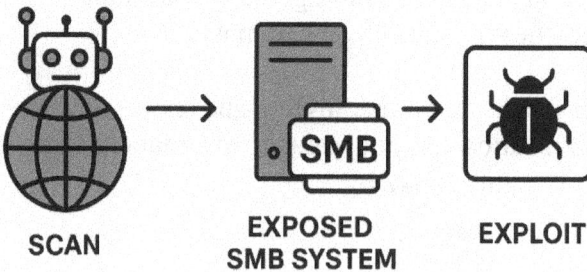

SCAN → EXPOSED SMB SYSTEM → EXPLOIT

The Real Costs of Believing the Myth

Failing to take cybersecurity seriously can lead to far more than just IT headaches. When an attack happens, it quickly becomes a business crisis.

Consequences SMBs often face:

- **Extended downtime** – Interrupting operations, fulfillment, and customer support
- **Lost revenue** – From halted business or clients leaving due to distrust
- **Legal and compliance penalties** – Especially if customer data is breached
- **Ransom payments** – Ranging from a few thousand to hundreds of thousands
- **Long-term brand damage** – Many small companies never fully recover

Common pitfall: Many SMBs have cyber insurance but fail to meet the minimum-security requirements, leaving them uncovered when they need it most.

What Attackers Actually Do: Real-World SMB Threats

Let's strip away the Hollywood-style cyberattack myths. In the real world, the vast majority of successful attacks on SMBs fall into a few predictable categories.

Common types of attacks targeting SMBs:

- **Phishing emails** that trick employees into clicking links or giving up passwords
- **Ransomware** that locks down files until a payment is made
- **Business Email Compromise (BEC)** where attackers impersonate executives to trick staff into wiring money
- **Credential stuffing** using leaked passwords from unrelated sites to access SMB systems

SMB-Targeted Attacks

Attack	Impact	Prevention
Phishing	Exposure of sensitive information	User training; email filtering
Ransomware	Data encryption; ransom demands	Regular backups; patching
Business Email Compromise	Financial loss via email fraud	Verify requests; 2FA
Credential Stuffing	Account takeover; data theft	Strong passwords; MFA

Real-World Case: A Small Firm, a Big Mistake

What happened: A 12-person architecture firm in the Midwest ignored IT upgrades for years. Thinking they were "too niche" to attract attackers, they operated with outdated software and had no offsite backups. One Monday morning, they were locked out of all files—hit by a ransomware attack. The ransom was $28,000.

What went wrong:

- They had no endpoint protection
- No employee had training on phishing recognition
- Their backup system hadn't worked in over six months

What we learn:

This wasn't a targeted attack—it was automated. The attackers didn't even know who the firm was. The firm ended up paying the ransom because client project files were at risk, and it took weeks to rebuild trust with clients.

How to Defend Yourself Without Breaking the Bank

You don't need a massive budget or a CISO to reduce your risk. But you do need a mindset shift—from reactive to proactive.

Tactical best practices:

- **Implement basic security hygiene**: Strong passwords, updates, and antivirus tools
- **Train employees regularly**: Phishing simulation and awareness sessions
- **Use cloud backups**: Ensure offsite, encrypted backups are taken frequently
- **Patch everything**: Especially routers, email systems, and remote access tools

Checklist to get started:

- Review current security tools and gaps
- Confirm daily or weekly backups are successful
- Create a simple incident response plan
- Schedule employee cybersecurity training
- Enable firewall and endpoint protection on all devices

Where Affordable Protections Can Be Applied for SMBs

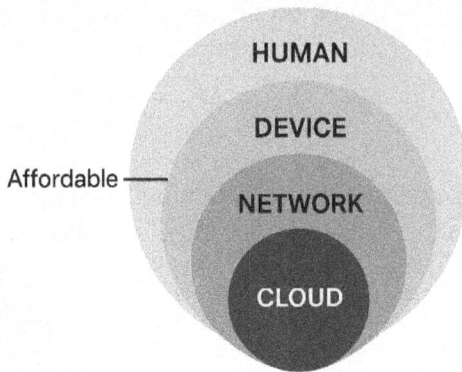

HUMAN

DEVICE

Affordable ——

NETWORK

CLOUD

Conclusion

The idea that "no one is coming after us" is not just outdated—it's dangerous. In a world of automated threats, SMBs are often the first ones hit and the last ones to recover. But this risk isn't unmanageable. With basic, scalable defenses, your business can become a hard target in a world full of easy ones.

Next Steps

Start by shifting your mindset. No business is too small for a cyberattack—but every business can make itself a harder target. In the next chapter, we tackle one of the most common and easily fixable vulnerabilities: weak passwords and the failure to use multi-factor authentication.

Up Next: *Chapter 2: Reusing Weak Passwords Without Multi-Factor Authentication*

Chapter 2: Reusing Weak Passwords Without Multi-Factor Authentication

Introduction

Passwords are still the front door to your business—and in far too many cases, that door is barely locked. Reused passwords. Short passwords. Easily guessed passwords. Worse still, passwords often stand alone with no additional form of protection.

This isn't just an IT oversight. It's the #1 cause of account takeovers, data leaks, and ransomware footholds. Cybercriminals rely on weak credentials because they work—and they know most SMBs aren't enforcing stronger alternatives.

In this chapter, we'll walk through how poor password hygiene and a lack of multi-factor authentication (MFA) expose your business, and what you can do—quickly and affordably—to fix it.

The Password Problem Most SMBs Ignore

Passwords haven't changed much since the '90s—but attackers have. Today, cybercriminals have access to billions of leaked passwords from previous breaches. They automate attacks using bots to test usernames and password combinations across thousands of websites and systems in minutes.

This is called **credential stuffing**, and it thrives on reused and weak passwords.

Why this issue persists:

- Employees reuse passwords across multiple tools
- SMBs often don't enforce minimum complexity or change policies
- MFA is seen as too complicated or time-consuming
- Many businesses underestimate just how easy it is to crack a weak password

Timeline of Password Cracking Speed

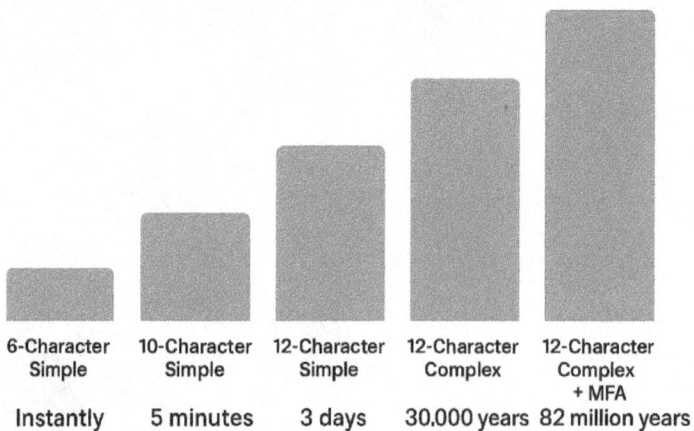

6-Character Simple	10-Character Simple	12-Character Simple	12-Character Complex	12-Character Complex + MFA
Instantly	5 minutes	3 days	30,000 years	82 million years

What Hackers Actually Do with Your Passwords

Once a single set of credentials is stolen—whether through phishing, malware, or a third-party breach—attackers don't just access that one account. They plug it into automated tools that attempt logins on:

- Email platforms (Outlook, Gmail)
- Cloud drives (OneDrive, Dropbox)
- Financial tools (QuickBooks, banking portals)
- Collaboration apps (Slack, Teams, Zoom)

And if those accounts are connected to administrative rights or payment systems, the results can be devastating.

Real-world consequences of weak passwords:

- Unauthorized money transfers
- Exposure of sensitive customer files
- Access to inboxes used for spear phishing
- Entry point for ransomware payloads

Real-World Case: One Password, Multiple Doors

What happened: A marketing agency with 18 employees suffered a breach when an intern reused their Gmail password for a project management tool. That password had been leaked in a separate breach two years earlier.

What went wrong:

- The password was reused across multiple platforms
- There was no MFA on the project management tool
- The attacker used that access to phish the agency's clients with malware-laced invoices

What we learn:

This wasn't a highly sophisticated attack. The attacker simply bought the leaked credentials and used them to test common tools. The agency spent over $40,000 recovering from client fallout and reputational damage.

How to Build Better Password Habits

You can't rely on employees to remember dozens of complex, unique passwords—and you don't have to. Instead, shift the responsibility to tools and policies that make secure behavior easy.

Tactical best practices:

- **Use a password manager**: Centralize and encrypt credential storage
- **Enforce unique passwords**: Require different passwords for different tools
- **Train staff on credential risks**: Show how hackers exploit reused or leaked credentials
- **Implement password policies**: Set minimum length and block weak combinations
- **Rotate passwords after exposure**: Use breach monitoring tools to detect leaks

The MFA Advantage: One Step That Changes Everything

Multi-Factor Authentication adds a second layer of protection beyond the password. Even if a password is stolen, access is blocked unless the second factor—like a text code, app prompt, or physical token—is also verified.

Types of MFA options:

- **SMS codes**: Sent to a mobile number
- **Authenticator apps**: Like Microsoft Authenticator or Google Authenticator
- **Hardware keys**: Physical devices like YubiKeys
- **Biometric options**: Fingerprint or facial recognition (where supported)

Checklist for rolling out MFA:

- Start with email, cloud storage, and financial platforms
- Require MFA for any administrative or privileged accounts
- Select an authenticator method appropriate for your team
- Test MFA enrollment with a small group before full rollout
- Document a fallback plan for lost devices or access

Comparring Different Types of MFA

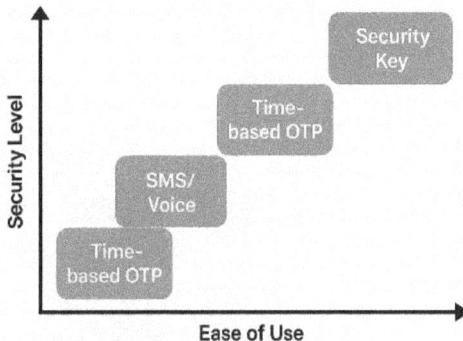

Security Level (y-axis), Ease of Use (x-axis)

- Time-based OTP
- SMS/Voice
- Time-based OTP
- Security Key

Conclusion

Weak and reused passwords are like open windows in your digital office. They might go unnoticed for weeks—until someone slips in and steals your most valuable data. Fortunately, this is one of the easiest vulnerabilities to fix. Strong password practices paired with MFA can stop the majority of automated attacks cold.

Next Steps

Take inventory of where your team stores and reuses passwords. Introduce a password manager and roll out MFA on high-risk platforms. These steps form the foundation of a strong security posture.

Next, we move from credential risks to another common entry point: deceptive emails. In the next chapter, we break down the phishing trap—and how one wrong click can take down your entire business.

Up Next: *Chapter 3: Clicking That One Wrong Link — The Phishing Trap*

Chapter 3: Clicking That One Wrong Link — The Phishing Trap

Introduction

You don't need a sophisticated hacker to breach your business—just one employee clicking the wrong link. Phishing remains the #1 delivery method for ransomware, business email compromise (BEC), and credential theft. And today's phishing emails aren't riddled with typos or coming from a sketchy overseas domain—they're polished, timely, and convincing.

For SMBs, this makes phishing one of the most dangerous and common entry points. In this chapter, we'll unpack how phishing works, what modern phishing campaigns actually look like, and most importantly, how to train your team to recognize and report suspicious activity before it becomes a business disaster.

Why Phishing Still Works So Well

Phishing works because it targets the human layer—the part of your business that can't be patched with software. Whether it's an urgent email from "the CEO," a fake invoice, or a security alert from a cloud provider, phishing relies on manipulation, not malware.

Tactics attackers use to trick users:

- Creating a sense of urgency ("Update your password immediately")
- Faking familiarity ("See attached invoice for your review")
- Impersonating known brands or internal contacts
- Embedding malware in attachments or links

Why SMBs are especially vulnerable:

- Teams wear many hats, making it easier to miss small details
- No formal training or phishing simulations
- Overreliance on spam filters or antivirus software

Breakdown of a Modern Phishing Email

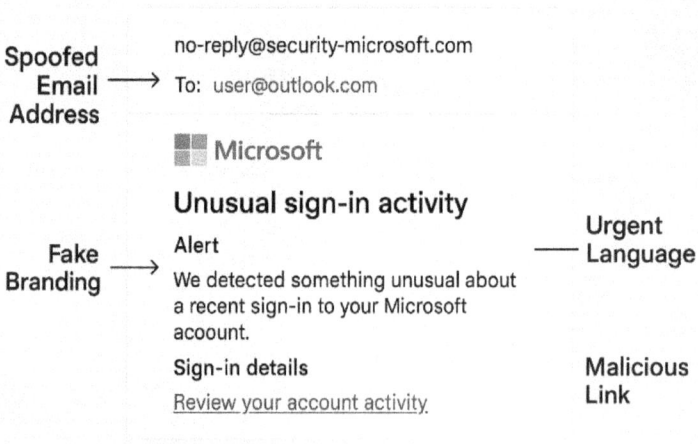

Spoofed Email Address → no-reply@security-microsoft.com
To: user@outlook.com

Microsoft

Unusual sign-in activity

Fake Branding →

Alert — Urgent Language

We detected something unusual about a recent sign-in to your Microsoft acoount.

Sign-in details

Review your account activity — Malicious Link

The Types of Phishing Attacks You Need to Know

Not all phishing attacks are created equal. They vary in complexity, delivery, and intent—but all aim to compromise access or trick users into taking dangerous action.

Common phishing techniques:

- **Email phishing**: The most widespread method—deceptive emails with fake links or attachments
- **Spear phishing**: Personalized emails targeting a specific individual or role, often using LinkedIn or social data
- **Smishing**: Phishing via SMS texts, often pretending to be from banks, delivery services, or IT teams
- **Voice phishing (vishing)**: Phone calls impersonating vendors, tech support, or executives

Comparison of Phishing Types

Phishing Type	Example	Delivery Method	Risk Level
Email Phishing	Your account will be suspended. Click here to verify."	Email	
Spear Phishing	Please review the attached invoice, John.	Email	
Smishing	Payment issue, call this number:	SMS	
Vishing	This is the IRS. You owe back taxes.	Phone Call	

Real-World Case: One Link, Total Lockdown

What happened: An office manager at a dental clinic received what looked like a DocuSign request from a known vendor. The email included branding, a familiar sender name, and a subject line referencing an actual invoice from a week prior. She clicked the link and entered her email login. Within hours, ransomware was launched across the network.

What went wrong:

- No user training or phishing awareness
- The email system had no alert for external senders impersonating internal accounts
- No MFA on the email account that was compromised

What we learn:

This wasn't a random attack—it was socially engineered. The attacker had done minimal research and mimicked previous communications. A simple phishing test and MFA could have stopped it cold.

How to Train Your Team to Spot the Bait

Your team is your first and last line of defense. With the right awareness and culture, employees can learn to recognize and report phishing attempts in seconds.

Tactical best practices:

- **Run regular phishing simulations**: Use real-world examples and test all staff
- **Teach the telltale signs**: Unknown senders, unexpected links, misspelled domains, urgent requests
- **Create a simple reporting process**: Make it easy to flag suspicious messages to IT
- **Celebrate "phish catches"**: Reinforce the behavior with recognition and feedback

Checklist for phishing prevention:

- Enable banner warnings for emails from external domains
- Use DNS filtering to block known malicious sites
- Implement email authentication (SPF, DKIM, DMARC)
- Add MFA to all email accounts
- Provide quarterly awareness refreshers and real-world examples

Layered Defense Against Phishing

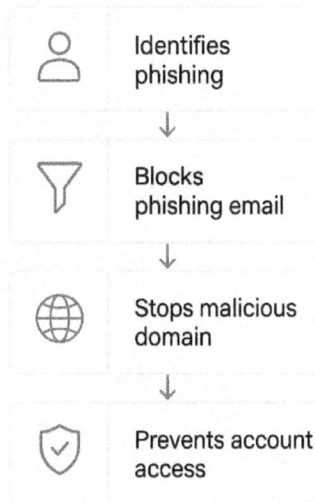

Identifies phishing

↓

Blocks phishing email

↓

Stops malicious domain

↓

Prevents account access

Conclusion

Phishing is cheap, fast, and incredibly effective—especially against SMBs with minimal awareness training. But with just a few smart changes in culture and technology, you can make your business a much harder target. The key isn't eliminating risk, it's empowering your people to recognize it.

Next Steps

Audit your inboxes and your inbox habits. Start phishing simulations and make reporting suspicious emails part of daily work life. And remember—technology fails fast when people aren't trained. That's where we're headed next: building a cyber-aware culture that reduces risk from the inside out.

Up Next: *Chapter 4: Skipping Cybersecurity Awareness for Your Team*

Chapter 4: Skipping Cybersecurity Awareness for Your Team

Introduction

You can invest in top-tier firewalls, endpoint protection, and cloud security tools—but if your team isn't trained to recognize threats, your business is still at risk. In fact, human error remains the leading cause of cybersecurity incidents across all industries, and small businesses are no exception.

Skipping cybersecurity awareness is like locking your front door and leaving the windows open. Without continuous education, even your most well-meaning employees can unintentionally expose your organization to costly attacks.

This chapter explores how to embed cybersecurity into your company culture, build training programs that stick, and run simulations that reduce internal risk without disrupting productivity.

The People Problem: Why Tools Alone Aren't Enough

Security software is essential—but it can only go so far. Many threats today are designed to bypass technical defenses by targeting human behavior. Whether it's clicking a phishing link, sharing sensitive info over a call, or using a weak password, attackers are counting on one thing: untrained users.

Common employee-related security gaps:

- Falling for phishing and social engineering scams
- Using personal devices without proper protections
- Sharing credentials or reusing weak passwords
- Mishandling sensitive data in email or cloud platforms

Why this matters:

- Your team is involved in every transaction, email, and access point
- Human error doesn't require a breach—it *is* the breach
- Training is one of the lowest-cost, highest-impact security investments

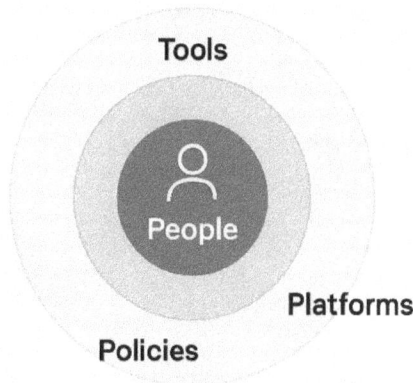

Building a Cyber-Aware Culture

Cybersecurity shouldn't be a once-a-year training—it should be part of everyday operations. A strong security culture turns every employee into an active participant in protecting the business.

What a cyber-aware team looks like:

- Staff pause before clicking unknown links or attachments
- Employees report suspicious behavior without fear
- Teams understand data sensitivity and access rights
- Cybersecurity is discussed regularly—not just when something breaks

How to build that culture:

- **Start at the top**: Leadership must model good cybersecurity habits
- **Make it routine**: Monthly micro-trainings, tips, and reminders
- **Celebrate wins**: Highlight staff who report phishing or fix missteps
- **Keep it relevant**: Tailor examples to your actual tools and industry

---

Real-World Case: Tools Were in Place—But People Weren't Ready

What happened: A logistics firm implemented enterprise-grade endpoint protection and MFA. But during a busy quarter, a new hire received a phishing email impersonating IT. It requested credentials for a "VPN upgrade." The employee responded, and attackers gained access to the internal network.

What went wrong:

- The employee had not yet received security training
- No simulation had been run to test user responses to fake IT requests
- The company assumed tools alone were enough

What we learn:

Technology worked—but human behavior undermined it. A simple awareness program could have prevented the breach, which cost the company weeks of downtime and nearly $100,000 in lost revenue and recovery costs.

Simulations That Stick: Training Without the Eye Rolls

Cybersecurity training doesn't have to be boring. The goal is engagement and retention—not lectures. Interactive, practical simulations are the most effective way to build muscle memory.

Tactical best practices:

- **Phishing simulations**: Send fake attacks to see who clicks and why
- **Role-based training**: Tailor content for finance, HR, or operations
- **Gamification**: Use quizzes, leaderboards, and prizes to drive engagement
- **Short and frequent beats long and rare**: 5 minutes a month > 2 hours a year

Checklist to launch a training program:

- Choose a cybersecurity training platform or provider
- Schedule quarterly simulations and awareness refreshers
- Track performance and report results to leadership
- Adjust content based on common mistakes or new threats
- Reinforce accountability with positive feedback

Phishing Simulation

Email sent → User clicks or reports → Feedback given → Metrics tracked

---

Conclusion

Every business says "people are our greatest asset"—but in cybersecurity, untrained people are also your greatest risk. By building a cyber-aware culture and running practical, engaging simulations, you dramatically lower your internal risk and strengthen every dollar spent on tech defenses.

Next Steps

Evaluate your current training efforts (or lack thereof). Start small—
one simulation, one tip, one team meeting—and build from there. A
security-conscious team can catch threats before they hit your
network.

In the next chapter, we take this awareness outside the office walls.
Remote work introduces a whole new attack surface—and it's time
to secure it.

Up Next: *Chapter 5: Assuming Remote Work Doesn't Increase Risk*

Chapter 5: Assuming Remote Work Doesn't Increase Risk

Introduction

The modern workplace is no longer confined to office walls. For SMBs, remote work offers flexibility, productivity, and access to a wider talent pool—but it also introduces new risks that many businesses overlook. When employees connect from home networks, use personal devices, or install unsanctioned apps, your security perimeter becomes fluid and fragile.

Assuming remote work doesn't increase risk is a mistake that cybercriminals love to exploit. This chapter outlines the key threats in a remote or hybrid setup—and how to secure your distributed team without killing convenience.

The Remote Work Risk Landscape

Before 2020, most SMB networks were built around a central office. Now, every employee's living room is a satellite of your digital infrastructure. That shift has radically expanded the attack surface.

Why remote work introduces new vulnerabilities:

- Home Wi-Fi networks often lack encryption or proper router security
- Personal devices may lack antivirus or up-to-date software
- File sharing via unsanctioned apps (Dropbox, Google Drive, WhatsApp)
- Increased phishing and social engineering targeting remote users

Common blind spots:

- No visibility into personal or mobile devices
- Employees using the same device for work, gaming, and family browsing
- Unsecured remote desktop tools like RDP or VPNs without MFA

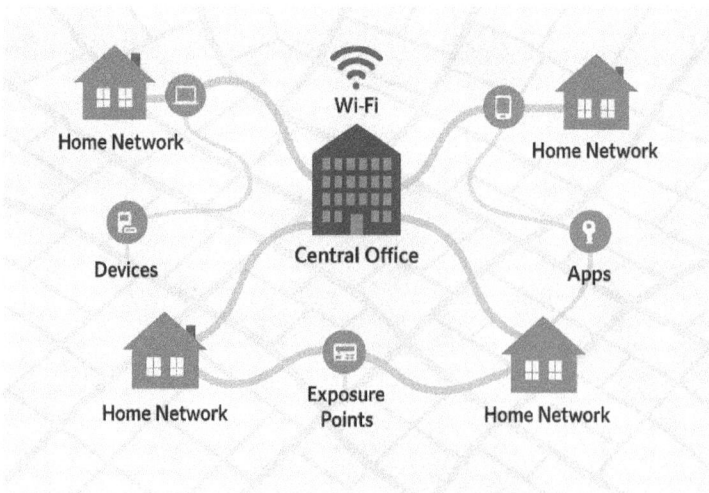

The Most Common Remote Work Mistakes

While remote work setups differ, the risks often stem from the same habits. Many SMBs unknowingly enable insecure behavior by prioritizing speed and convenience over policy.

What not to do:

- Allow remote access without MFA or endpoint protection
- Let users connect over public Wi-Fi without a secure VPN
- Ignore mobile device security (especially for email and file sharing)
- Rely on employees to "figure it out" when setting up their home systems

High-risk remote access tools:

- Unsecured VPN tunnels with static credentials
- Remote Desktop Protocol (RDP) exposed to the internet
- File transfer tools that bypass corporate cloud storage

Real-World Case: A Small Team, a Big Backdoor

What happened: A 10-person consulting firm moved fully remote. To make things easy, the owner enabled RDP access for all employees. No MFA. No network segmentation. An attacker scanned the internet, found an exposed RDP port, and brute-forced a weak password. Within minutes, they had access to the owner's desktop and financial systems.

What went wrong:

- No MFA or VPN to protect remote connections
- Reused passwords that were already exposed in a previous breach
- No monitoring in place to detect abnormal access

What we learn:

Remote access without layered security is an open door. The attacker didn't target the firm—they found them automatically via an IP scan. Simple safeguards like VPN + MFA would have prevented the breach entirely.

Securing the Home Office Without Killing Productivity

Security shouldn't slow people down. Instead, it should support productive, flexible work while minimizing risk. It starts by standardizing remote access and securing devices.

Tactical best practices:

- **Mandate MFA on all remote logins**
- **Use business-grade VPNs** with endpoint checks and logging
- **Deploy endpoint protection** across all work-from-home devices
- **Control access to company data** via cloud permissions and DLP tools
- **Limit shadow IT** by listing approved apps and flagging high-risk ones

Checklist to secure remote teams:

- Inventory all tools used outside the office
- Require approved VPN for any system access
- Add antivirus/EDR to employee laptops and phones
- Educate users on secure home Wi-Fi setup (WPA3, router updates)
- Enforce mobile device management (MDM) for BYOD policies

✓ VPN **VPN**

✓ 🔒 **MFA**

✓ 🛡 **Endpoint Security**

✓ 📶 **Wi-Fi Settings**

✓ ☁ **Cloud Access Controls**

Conclusion

Remote work isn't going away—but neither are the risks it brings. The key isn't pulling everyone back to the office. It's understanding where your perimeter has shifted and how to secure it with scalable, user-friendly protections.

Next Steps

Start by mapping out who is connecting, from where, and with what. Lock down remote access points with MFA and endpoint protection. And don't wait until a breach to realize the importance of patching, which brings us to our next chapter: why delaying software updates can undo everything you've secured so far.

Up Next: *Chapter 6: Delaying Security Updates and Patches*

Part II: Technology & Configuration Mistakes

Chapter 6: Delaying Security Updates and Patches

Introduction

Every day you delay a security update is a day your business is vulnerable. Cybercriminals actively scan the internet for outdated software, plugins, and systems—and once a vulnerability is published, it's only a matter of time before someone tries to exploit it.

Skipping patches doesn't just leave the back door open—it removes the door entirely. Yet many SMBs delay updates for fear of disrupting operations or because they don't have a process in place. In this chapter, we'll show why patching is critical, how unpatched systems are exploited, and how to create a simple, automated update process that keeps your business secure.

The Cost of Falling Behind on Patching

Cybercriminals don't need to guess how to break into your systems. They just read the patch notes. Public vulnerability disclosures often include exact details on the flaw—and attackers move quickly to exploit businesses that haven't applied the fix.

Why patches matter:

- Most ransomware attacks exploit known, unpatched vulnerabilities
- Many exploits are available online as ready-to-use scripts
- Cloud platforms, browsers, and CRMs are frequent targets
- Delays create a widening gap between your defenses and active threats

Common excuses SMBs make:

- "It's working fine, we'll update later"
- "We're afraid the update might break something"
- "We don't have time to test everything after an update"
- "We thought our provider was handling that"

Shrinking patching window

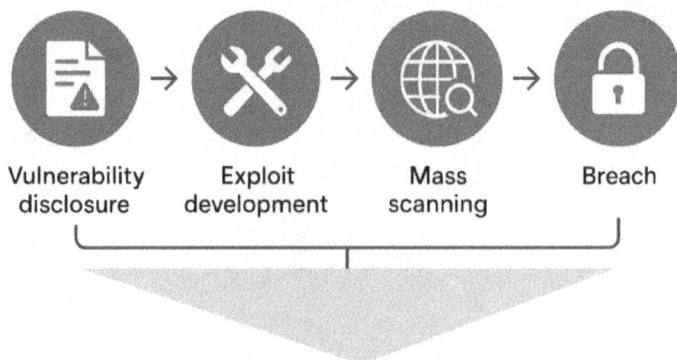

| Vulnerability disclosure | Exploit development | Mass scanning | Breach |

Where Unpatched Systems Hide

Patching isn't just about Windows updates. Many attacks happen through third-party tools, outdated firmware, or forgotten apps that quietly create vulnerabilities.

Frequently overlooked updates:

- WordPress plugins and CMS platforms
- Remote access tools and VPN software
- Printer firmware and IoT devices
- Chrome/Edge browser versions
- Collaboration platforms like Zoom, Teams, Slack

Attackers look for:

- Known CVEs (Common Vulnerabilities and Exposures)
- Outdated libraries in web apps
- Unpatched software with elevated privileges
- Weak legacy systems still connected to the network

Real-World Case: The Patch That Came Too Late

What happened: A regional accounting firm used an outdated version of a PDF viewer with a known remote code execution flaw. The vendor had released a patch six weeks earlier, but no one had applied it. A malicious PDF attached to a phishing email triggered the exploit, giving attackers direct access to the firm's file server.

What went wrong:

- No automated patch management in place
- No inventory of installed applications
- Users had admin rights, allowing the exploit to run freely

What we learn:

Even low-profile tools can become entry points. If your patching depends on manual tracking, something will get missed. Automation and visibility are non-negotiable.

How to Patch Smarter (and Faster)

The key to effective patching isn't speed alone—it's consistency. Businesses that succeed don't rely on users to install updates. They automate where possible and schedule downtime for critical systems.

Tactical best practices:

- **Centralize patch management** with an RMM (Remote Monitoring and Management) or MDM platform
- **Run weekly scans** for missing patches and updates
- **Test updates in a staging environment** for critical applications
- **Automate third-party updates** (e.g., Chrome, Adobe, Zoom)
- **Track and report on patch status** to ensure compliance

Checklist to improve patch hygiene:

- Maintain an up-to-date software inventory
- Subscribe to vendor security bulletins
- Set auto-updates where possible for browsers and office tools
- Schedule monthly patch windows for OS and critical apps
- Use vulnerability scanning tools to audit for missed patches

Patch Status

System	Update Age	Priority
■ Servers	Current	● Low
■ Desktops	30 + days	● High
▒ Laptops	7 days	● Medium
■ Network devices	14 days	● Medium

Conclusion

Delaying updates isn't a harmless inconvenience—it's a time bomb.
Most attacks exploit issues that already have fixes available. If
you're not patching, you're gambling, and for many SMBs, the odds
run out fast. But the fix is straightforward: automate, prioritize, and
make patching a non-negotiable part of your operational routine.

Next Steps

Assess your current patching process. What's being updated
regularly—and what's not? Implement automation tools and develop
a clear policy for testing and applying patches across systems.

Next, we'll focus on another wide-open door: exposed admin panels
and open ports—some of the easiest ways attackers get in.

Up Next: *Chapter 7: Leaving Admin Panels and Ports Publicly
Exposed*

Chapter 7: Leaving Admin Panels and Ports Publicly Exposed

Introduction

Every second, automated bots scan the internet for open ports, default login pages, and unprotected admin panels. If your business is leaving those doors wide open—without firewall rules, IP restrictions, or access controls—you're inviting attackers into your infrastructure.

Admin portals are often the most privileged part of your system, yet in many SMBs, they're left exposed due to poor defaults, misconfigurations, or lack of visibility. This chapter explains how these exposures happen, what hackers look for, and how you can lock down your environment with simple, scalable protections.

Why Admin Panels Are a Favorite Target

Admin portals give full control: user access, payment data, system settings—everything. Cybercriminals know that many SMBs never change default settings or properly configure access controls.

How attackers find open panels:

- Use of tools like Shodan to scan IP ranges for open ports
- Exploiting common platforms (e.g., WordPress, cPanel, NAS dashboards)
- Checking for login pages at standard URLs like /admin or /wp-login.php
- Testing default credentials or brute-force passwords

Common exposure mistakes:

- Leaving remote desktop access (RDP) or SSH open to the internet
- Using public-facing panels without IP restrictions or VPN
- Relying solely on weak login credentials with no MFA
- Hosting control panels on default ports (e.g., 22, 3389, 443)

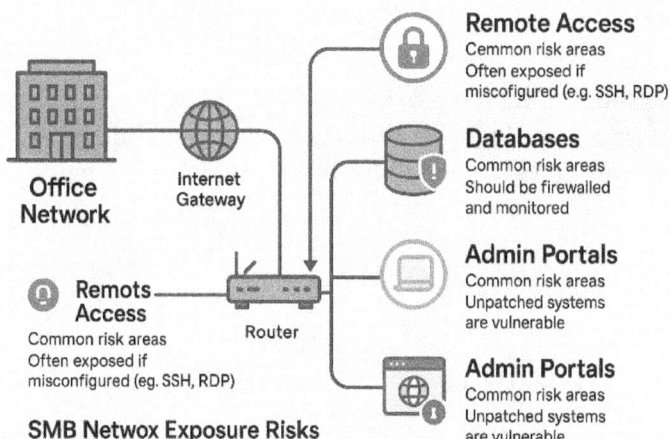

Remote Access
Cemmon risk areas
Often exposed if
miscofigured (e.g. SSH, RDP)

Databases
Common risk areas
Should be firewalled
and monitored

Admin Portals
Common risk areas
Unpatched systems
are vulnerable

Admin Portals
Common risk areas
Unpatched systems
are vulnerable

Office Network

Internet Gateway

Remots Access
Common risk areas
Often exposed if
misconfigured (eg. SSH, RDP)

Router

SMB Netwox Exposure Risks

Real-World Case: Small Server, Big Breach

What happened: A small e-commerce shop hosted its own site and database using a popular control panel. The admin login was available via the default web address and had no access restrictions. Attackers discovered it using a basic Shodan scan, brute-forced the password, and gained access to the customer database.

What went wrong:

- Admin panel was exposed directly to the internet
- Login was protected only by a weak password
- No firewall or IP whitelisting in place

What we learn:

Hackers didn't need a zero-day—they just needed five minutes and basic tools. This type of exposure is shockingly common, but just as easily preventable.

Locking the Doors: Best Practices for Securing Access Points

When it comes to admin panels and ports, your strategy should be simple: *make them invisible or require proof before access*. If a system doesn't need to be public-facing, it shouldn't be.

Tactical best practices:

- **Use a VPN or zero-trust gateway** for all admin interfaces
- **Change default ports** for remote access tools and admin panels
- **Restrict access by IP address or geolocation**
- **Enforce MFA on every panel, not just email**
- **Disable unused services and close non-essential ports**

Checklist to secure public-facing infrastructure:

- Run a port scan on your own IP range (using Nmap or similar)
- Change default admin URLs and ports
- Enforce strict firewall rules for inbound connections
- Require VPN or SSO for internal tools and dashboards
- Audit cloud dashboards and services for public exposure

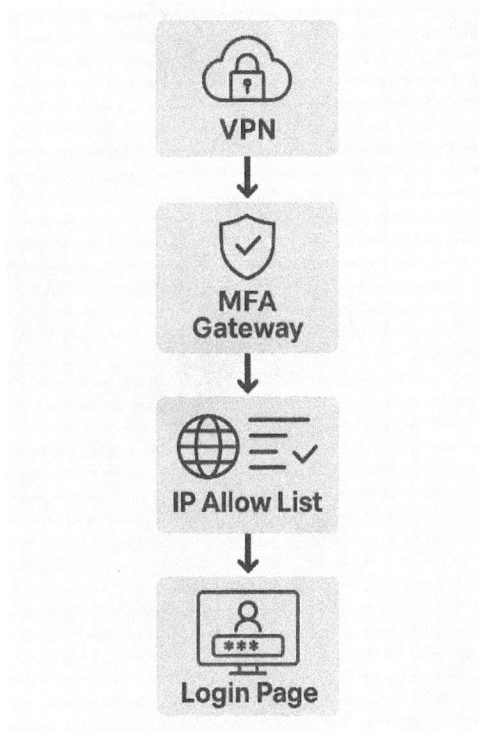

VPN

↓

MFA Gateway

↓

IP Allow List

↓

Login Page

Conclusion

Hackers aren't hunting for your business specifically—they're scanning for easy access. Leaving ports and panels open to the public is like leaving keys in the door. With a few configuration changes and better access controls, you can lock down your most sensitive systems and become an invisible target.

Next Steps

Audit your infrastructure using a basic port scanner. Close what isn't needed, restrict what is, and never assume a hidden URL is secure. In the next chapter, we explore another core security pillar: encryption—what it protects, and how to use it to safeguard customer trust.

Up Next: *Chapter 8: Failing to Encrypt Customer and Internal Data*

Chapter 8: Failing to Encrypt Customer and Internal Data

Introduction

You wouldn't hand out your customers' personal data on paper—but if you're not encrypting it digitally, that's essentially what you're doing. Unencrypted data is readable by anyone who gains access—whether through a stolen device, compromised cloud account, or intercepted communication.

Encryption turns sensitive data into unreadable code—useless to attackers without the key. It's one of the simplest, most powerful protections you can implement—and one of the most commonly skipped steps by SMBs.

In this chapter, we'll explore why encryption matters, where it should be applied, and how to make it part of your everyday business processes.

What Happens When You Skip Encryption

Encryption isn't just for banks and tech giants. It's critical for any business storing:

- Customer contact details
- Payment information
- Employee records
- Legal contracts
- Intellectual property

Common failure points:

- Unencrypted laptops or USB drives that get lost or stolen
- Cloud storage files that are shared without encryption
- Emails sent with sensitive attachments in plain text
- Applications storing passwords or data without secure hashing

The consequences:

- Data leaks become legal liabilities (especially under GDPR, HIPAA, or state privacy laws)
- Exposed records damage customer trust and lead to lost contracts
- Insurance claims may be denied if encryption wasn't used

ENCRYPTED DATA	UNENCRYPTED DATA
K77$k✕XE@i [9a&UlQw* 2z+H!t3# =b44mP0_jd	Customer name 1234 Elm St. Account number Order details

Real-World Case: Laptop Lost, Data Exposed

What happened: An employee at a boutique real estate firm left their company-issued laptop in a rideshare vehicle. The device wasn't encrypted and was logged into both email and a CRM system containing customer financial records. Within days, identity theft reports surfaced among clients.

What went wrong:

- No disk encryption was enabled
- No auto-lock or remote wipe features in place
- Sensitive client data was stored locally and accessible without a password

What we learn:

Encryption could have made the laptop useless to the thief. Instead, it became a liability event that cost the firm six figures in damages and lost reputation.

Where and How to Use Encryption

Encryption should be layered—not limited to one part of your system. Think of it as a seatbelt for your data: always on, always protecting, even when things go wrong.

Tactical best practices:

- **Enable full-disk encryption** on all laptops and mobile devices (e.g., BitLocker, FileVault)
- **Use encrypted email solutions** or secure portals for sensitive communication
- **Encrypt databases and backups** with managed keys
- **Avoid sending passwords or client data over unsecured channels**
- **Use end-to-end encryption** for messaging and collaboration tools

Checklist for encryption hygiene:

- Confirm full-disk encryption is enabled across all devices
- Audit cloud storage for file-level encryption and sharing settings
- Implement encrypted backups, both on-prem and in the cloud
- Use secure email plugins or web portals for client-facing communication
- Rotate and manage encryption keys securely

ENCRYPTION

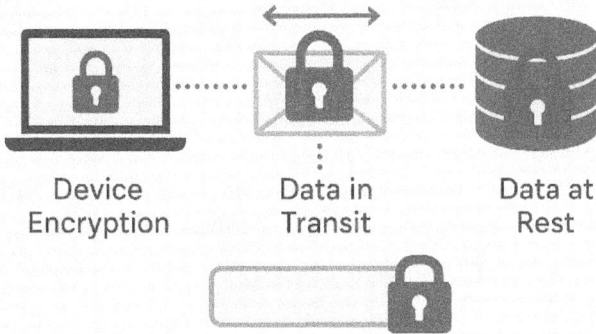

| Device Encryption | Data in Transit | Data at Rest |

Conclusion

Encryption doesn't prevent a breach—but it renders the stolen data useless. It's one of the clearest ways to reduce legal risk, maintain trust, and prove due diligence in today's privacy-first landscape. For SMBs, encryption isn't a luxury—it's a baseline.

Next Steps

Evaluate your current use of encryption. Start with devices and backups, then secure email and cloud storage. If you're not encrypting sensitive data, you're gambling with more than just information—you're risking your entire business reputation.

Next, we'll look at another critical mistake: Assuming your cloud provider provides handless security.

Up Next: *Chapter 9: Assuming your cloud provider handless security*

Chapter 9: Assuming Your Cloud Provider Handles Security

Introduction

The cloud doesn't come with built-in security—it comes with shared responsibility. One of the most dangerous assumptions an SMB can make is believing that their cloud provider (like AWS, Azure, or Google Cloud) is securing everything for them. The truth is, cloud vendors secure the *infrastructure*—but your *data*, *user access*, and *configuration* are all on you.

Misconfigurations in the cloud are one of the leading causes of data breaches. This chapter breaks down what you're actually responsible for in the cloud, how attackers exploit common setup mistakes, and how to secure your cloud environment without needing a full-time DevOps team.

What Cloud Providers Do and Don't Protect

The cloud follows a shared responsibility model. That means the vendor protects the data center and core infrastructure, but you must secure your use of it.

Provider responsibilities (e.g., AWS, Azure, Google Cloud):

- Physical data center security
- Network infrastructure and hardware
- Hypervisor and core cloud services uptime

Your responsibilities as the customer:

- Secure identity and access management (IAM)
- Data encryption and storage policies
- Configuration of apps, virtual machines, databases, and firewalls
- Monitoring and logging activity

Biggest misunderstanding: SMBs assume enabling a cloud service means it's secure by default—it's not.

SHARED RESPONSIBILITY MODEL	
Managed by Provider	**Managed by Customer**
Physical Security	Identity & Access Management
Network Security	Data
Host Infrastructure	Applications
Applications	Operating System
	Network Configuration

How Cloud Misconfigurations Lead to Real Breaches

Misconfigured cloud environments are among the easiest attack surfaces for cybercriminals to exploit. These are not zero-days—they're wide-open doors.

Common SMB misconfigurations:

- Public S3 buckets exposing customer files
- Admin panels or storage accounts with no IP restrictions
- Overly permissive IAM roles (e.g., "admin" rights to all users)
- Logging turned off—so no one knows when something goes wrong

What attackers look for:

- Open ports or dashboards indexed in search engines
- Public links to private cloud files (images, PDFs, backups)
- Default credentials on cloud databases or services
- Forgotten or orphaned services still accepting requests

Real-World Case: Public Bucket, Private Disaster

What happened: A small online learning startup stored course videos and customer data in an AWS S3 bucket. But the bucket was accidentally marked as public. The data—including full names, emails, and payment receipts—was indexed by search engines and scraped by bots. The firm didn't notice until customers complained about seeing their data on pastebin sites.

What went wrong:

- Misconfigured storage settings
- No encryption or access logging
- No alerts set up for bucket policy changes

What we learn:

Cloud breaches don't require hacking—just missteps. Simple configuration errors can expose thousands of records in seconds.

How to Secure Your Cloud Environment

Securing the cloud isn't about complexity—it's about clarity. You need visibility, control, and smart defaults.

Tactical best practices:

- **Enable logging and alerting** (e.g., AWS CloudTrail, Azure Monitor)
- **Audit access controls regularly** – Remove unused accounts and tighten IAM roles
- **Encrypt data at rest and in transit**
- **Restrict access by IP, role, and region**
- **Use multi-factor authentication for cloud consoles**

Checklist for cloud security hygiene:

- Review your shared responsibility model with each vendor
- Run a configuration audit (AWS Config, GCP Security Command Center)
- Lock down public-facing services (buckets, ports, consoles)
- Set up monitoring and alerting for any changes
- Limit permissions using least privilege access

IAM

ENCRYPTION

CLOUD SECURITY CONTROLS

LOGGING

ACCESS CONTROLS

MONITORING

Conclusion

Cloud computing is powerful, flexible, and scalable—but it's not secure by default. You can't outsource responsibility for your data. Understanding and actively managing your part of the cloud equation is critical to protecting your business from invisible yet highly preventable threats.

Next Steps

Log into your cloud console and review what's publicly accessible. Set alerts for changes, scan your IAM roles, and confirm that data is encrypted. In the next chapter, we tackle a growing blind spot in the digital age: the improper use of AI tools and how they can inadvertently leak sensitive information.

Up Next: *Chapter 10: Using AI Tools Without Restricting Data Access*

Chapter 10: Using AI Tools Without Restricting Data Access

Introduction

AI tools like ChatGPT, Google Bard, and Microsoft Copilot are revolutionizing how businesses work—but they also introduce new risks. Many SMB employees copy-paste sensitive data, internal documents, or even customer records into these tools without realizing that it could violate privacy policies, regulatory obligations, or even leak intellectual property.

The problem isn't the AI—it's how we use it. This chapter unpacks the hidden risks of AI misuse, how data can be unintentionally exposed, and how to build privacy-aware workflows that leverage AI safely and responsibly.

What Happens When You Share Too Much with AI

When you paste data into an AI system, you're often sending that information to third-party servers—outside your business control. Even if tools are secure, data sent to them may be stored, logged, or processed in ways you can't fully control.

Risks of unregulated AI use:

- Leaking personally identifiable information (PII)
- Exposing sensitive business documents or source code
- Violating NDAs or compliance obligations
- Creating long-term data retention on external servers

Hidden exposure points:

- Staff pasting internal reports into AI prompts
- Using AI to summarize sensitive emails or contracts
- Uploading product roadmaps, client lists, or financial models

---

Real-World Case: The AI Prompt That Broke Trust

What happened: An employee at a small legal consultancy used ChatGPT to summarize confidential client correspondence. Unbeknownst to them, this data was processed and temporarily cached by the AI platform. Later, a similar query by another user surfaced phrasing that closely resembled the confidential text. The client found out—and terminated their contract.

What went wrong:

- No policy governing AI tool use
- Sensitive content shared in plaintext
- No restrictions on tool access or data retention

What we learn:

Even powerful tools can create powerful damage if used without boundaries. AI tools must be treated with the same privacy guardrails as any third-party data processor.

How to Use AI Without Creating Risk

AI can be a competitive advantage—but only when used responsibly. With the right policies and technical controls, you can empower your team to benefit from AI without exposing your business.

Tactical best practices:

- **Prohibit input of sensitive data** into public AI platforms
- **Use privacy-focused enterprise AI tools** with internal hosting or clear retention policies
- **Train staff on what's acceptable to share**
- **Mask or anonymize data before submission**
- **Log and review prompt history** when possible

Checklist for AI-safe usage:

- Create an internal policy for AI usage and data sensitivity
- Restrict access to public AI tools on company devices
- Offer approved internal AI systems (e.g., private LLMs)
- Conduct quarterly audits of AI-related activity
- Train staff on red flags and best practices

AI SAFETY CHECKLIST

Safe	Not Safe
✓ Ask for help summarizing a generic email	✗ Paste client contract
✓ Learn about general sales strategies	✗ Upload internal sales report
✓ Get ideas for a blog post topic	✗ Include confidential information
✓ Brainstorm names for a new product	✗ Process customer payment data

Conclusion

AI is here to stay—but so are the risks. The speed and intelligence it offers must be matched with responsibility. When your team knows what to avoid and has the right tools, AI becomes a strength—not a liability.

Next Steps

Review who in your company is using AI tools—and how. Define clear guidelines and make sure sensitive data never makes it into an AI prompt window. In the next chapter, we shift from digital behavior to backups.

Up Next: *Not Backing Up Critical Systems (or Not Testing Restores)*

Part III: Strategic, Compliance, and Recovery Mistakes

Chapter 11: Not Backing Up Critical Systems (or Not Testing Restores)

Introduction

It's easy to assume your data is safe just because you have a "backup system" in place. But for many small and mid-sized businesses (SMBs), that sense of safety is dangerously misleading. The truth is, unless backups are both **comprehensive** and **tested regularly**, you may find yourself facing total data loss when disaster strikes. From ransomware and hardware failures to human error and rogue updates, the risk scenarios are real—and far more common than you might think.

In this chapter, we'll break down what it means to truly protect your data, how to ensure backups are working when it counts, and why restore testing is the single most overlooked step in modern business continuity.

Why Backups Fail When You Need Them Most

A backup is only useful if it's recent, complete, and retrievable. Sadly, many businesses discover too late that theirs are none of these.

The Illusion of a Safety Net

There's a big difference between believing you have a backup and actually having one that works. Too often, backup systems are:

- Misconfigured or incomplete (missing key databases or applications)
- Stored on the same network that gets compromised
- Outdated due to failed backup jobs that went unnoticed
- Unrecoverable due to corrupt files or missing encryption keys

Backup Chain Failure Points

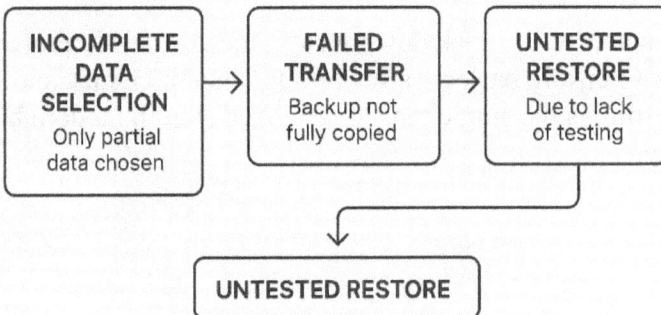

```
┌──────────────┐     ┌──────────────┐     ┌──────────────┐
│ INCOMPLETE   │     │   FAILED     │     │  UNTESTED    │
│    DATA      │ ──> │  TRANSFER    │ ──> │  RESTORE     │
│  SELECTION   │     │ Backup not   │     │ Due to lack  │
│ Only partial │     │ fully copied │     │ of testing   │
│ data chosen  │     │              │     │              │
└──────────────┘     └──────────────┘     └──────────────┘
                            │
                            ▼
                   ┌──────────────────┐
                   │ UNTESTED RESTORE │
                   └──────────────────┘
```

Silent Failures in "Set and Forget" Systems

Automated backups are incredibly helpful—but dangerous if left unchecked. Systems fail silently, notifications get ignored, and months can pass before anyone realizes something broke.

Essential Elements of a Reliable Backup Strategy

Protecting your business starts with knowing exactly what needs to be backed up, how often, and where it lives. Just as important: knowing how to get it all back fast.

The 3-2-1 Backup Rule (Still Works)

This widely respected guideline helps SMBs build resilient backup strategies:

- **3** total copies of your data
- **2** stored on different types of media (e.g., disk and cloud)
- **1** copy stored offsite (or offline)

Backup Frequency: Match It to Your Risk

- **Daily** backups for systems with regular changes (CRM, ERP, financials)
- **Hourly or real-time** for critical systems (e-commerce platforms, POS)
- **Weekly or monthly** for static archives or infrequently used data

Cloud vs. Local: Use Both

Relying on one method alone—just cloud or just local—is risky. Hybrid backups combine fast local restores with the disaster-resilience of cloud storage.

Why Testing Restores Is Non-Negotiable

If you haven't tested your backups, you don't have backups. Restore testing is the only way to know for sure that your recovery process works.

What Can Go Wrong in a Restore?

- Missing files or incomplete backups
- Backup encrypted but password/key is lost
- Software version mismatch (can't restore into new app version)
- Corrupted backup media

How Often Should You Test?

- **Monthly test** a partial restore from your most critical system
- **Quarterly full restore** simulation (non-production environment)
- **Annual disaster recovery drill** (restore entire business from scratch)

RESTORE TESTING CALENDAR

MONTHLY   QUARTERLY   ANNUAL

Common Pitfalls to Avoid

1. Assuming SaaS apps are fully backed up
Many assume platforms like Microsoft 365, Google Workspace, or Salesforce handle backups for them. They don't. These services offer some redundancy—but not full backup capabilities or point-in-time restores.

2. Forgetting to include configurations and system states
Backing up just the data isn't enough. You need system settings, virtual machines, and application configurations to restore full functionality.

3. Failing to secure your backups
Backups are a common ransomware target. If your backup is on the same network, it can be encrypted or deleted just like everything else.

Tactical Best Practices for SMBs

- Perform regular **automated backups** and manual validation
- Keep at least one copy **offline or air-gapped**
- Use **backup monitoring** with alerts for failed jobs
- Include **third-party SaaS data** in your strategy
- **Encrypt** backup files and store keys separately
- Test **restores from multiple points in time**, not just the latest

Real-World Example: When the Backups Didn't Work

What Happened
A mid-sized legal firm in the Midwest was hit by ransomware during a holiday weekend. Confident in their nightly backups, they declined to pay the ransom.

What Went Wrong
Their backups were stored on the same network that got encrypted. Worse, the system hadn't flagged that the last successful backup was over 10 days old. When they tried to restore, the files were corrupted.

What We Learn

- Never store backups on the same infrastructure as production
- Always monitor and **verify** backup job success
- Test restores regularly—**before** you're in crisis

FAILED BACKUP	BEST-PRACTICE BACKUP
❌ No offsite or cloud copy	✅ Has offsite or cloud copy
❌ Infrequent or irregular	✅ Frequent and regular
❌ Single local device or drive	✅ Redundant local+remote

Conclusion

Backups are the foundation of your disaster recovery plan—but only if they're done right. You must think beyond simply having backups to ensuring they're reliable, secure, and retrievable. Without this, you're gambling with the future of your business every day.

Next Steps

Review your current backup policy immediately. If you don't have one, start with the 3-2-1 rule and test your first restore this month. Get buy-in from leadership—it's not just an IT issue, it's a business survival issue.

In the next chapter, we'll tackle a closely related vulnerability: what to do when an incident actually hits. If you don't have an incident response plan, you're already behind.

Next: Chapter 12 – Operating Without an Incident Response Plan

Chapter 12: Operating Without an Incident Response Plan

Introduction

Every business will face a cyber incident. It might be a ransomware attack, a data breach, a phishing scam, or a system outage triggered by internal error. What separates damage control from disaster is not what happened — it's how prepared you were to respond. Yet countless small and mid-sized businesses (SMBs) are operating without a clear, tested incident response plan.

This chapter delivers what every SMB leader needs to know: how to recognize an incident fast, contain the damage, communicate effectively, and recover without chaos — even if you don't have a large IT team.

The Cost of Not Being Ready

An incident you can't respond to is an incident that controls you. Without a plan, your team is left guessing at a time when speed, clarity, and coordination are critical.

Why Minutes Matter

Delays in identifying and responding to an attack increase:

- **Data loss** and operational downtime
- **Financial exposure** from ransom demands or service disruption
- **Reputation damage** from poor customer communication
- **Legal and regulatory risk** from unreported or mishandled breaches

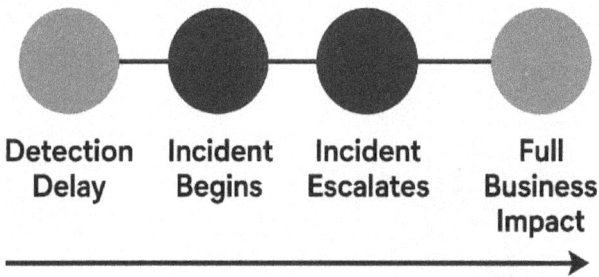

Detection Delay   Incident Begins   Incident Escalates   Full Business Impact

How Small Teams Get Overwhelmed

When there's no plan:

- No one knows who's in charge
- Critical decisions are made under pressure
- Legal, customer, and internal communications are inconsistent or missing
- External help (like forensic analysts or breach counsel) is called too late

---

Core Components of an Incident Response Plan

A good plan turns panic into process. It doesn't have to be complex, but it must be **clear, documented, and practiced**.

1. Define What an "Incident" Is

Start with clear triggers. Not everything is a breach, but these scenarios should launch a response:

- Suspicious login attempts or account takeovers
- Malware or ransomware detection
- System or data access anomalies
- Unusual outbound data flows
- Customer or employee reports of compromise

2. Assign Roles and Responsibilities

Even a three-person team can be effective — if roles are clear. Typical roles include:

- **Incident lead**: Coordinates response efforts
- **Communications lead**: Manages internal/external updates
- **IT/security lead**: Executes technical response (containment, analysis)

Create a simple **call tree** to escalate when needed.

3. Establish a Response Workflow

Document a step-by-step plan:

- **Identify and confirm** the incident
- **Contain** the threat (disconnect systems, limit access)
- **Preserve evidence** for legal and forensic use
- **Notify stakeholders** (internal teams, customers, legal, regulators)
- **Remediate** and restore systems
- **Review and document** the event for lessons learned

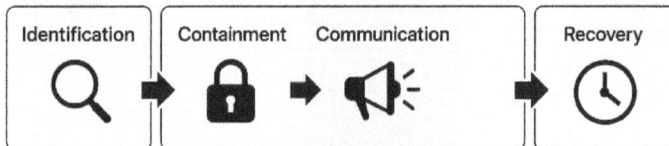

| Identification | Containment | Communication | Recovery |

Tactical Best Practices for SMBs

- Maintain a **simple response playbook** with key contacts and checklists
- Use **pre-written templates** for incident notifications
- Keep a **print copy** in case systems are inaccessible
- Run **tabletop exercises** at least twice per year
- Ensure **legal, IT, and leadership** have aligned expectations

---

Common Pitfalls to Avoid

1. Confusing response with prevention
Having firewalls and antivirus is not the same as knowing what to do when they fail.

2. Keeping the plan in someone's head
Plans that live only in one employee's brain (or inbox) won't help when they're on vacation—or when they're the victim of the attack.

3. Failing to test the plan
Even simple drills reveal missing pieces: wrong phone numbers, outdated tools, unclear responsibilities.

4. Ignoring communication
The technical fix is just one part of the response. Clear communication with staff, clients, and regulators is equally important.

Real-World Example: Chaos After a Ransomware Hit

What Happened

A boutique accounting firm suffered a ransomware attack during tax season. Files were encrypted, and the attackers demanded $80,000 in Bitcoin. The firm had no response plan, and their IT provider was unreachable.

What Went Wrong

- Internal staff didn't know whether to shut down systems
- No one contacted clients or regulators until days later
- The firm accidentally deleted logs needed for insurance and law enforcement
- Restoring from backups took over two weeks due to poor documentation

What We Learn

- Incident plans don't need to be perfect — they just need to exist
- Communication must be ready *before* the crisis
- Every hour without direction multiplies the damage

WITH PLAN	WITHOUT PLAN
Faster time to restore	Longer time to restore
Minimal reputation impact	Significant reputation damage
Few if any clients lost	Many clients lost

Checklist: Your SMB Incident Response Plan

Use this as your minimum baseline:

- ☑ Defined what qualifies as an "incident" for your org
- ☑ Assigned clear roles (lead, comms, tech)
- ☑ Documented a basic workflow from detection to resolution
- ☑ Stored copies offline and shared with leadership
- ☑ Created notification templates for staff and clients
- ☑ Practiced with a mock scenario in the last 6 months

Conclusion

Having an incident response plan isn't optional — it's foundational. Without it, your business is vulnerable to chaos, confusion, and catastrophic delays. With it, you can respond decisively, limit damage, and show customers, partners, and regulators that you're in control.

Next Steps

Gather your core team and spend one hour drafting your first incident response playbook. Start simple. Name roles, set triggers, and define your escalation path. Practice once a quarter — it will pay off tenfold when it counts.

In the next chapter, we'll address another silent threat: thinking you're exempt from cybersecurity compliance because you're not regulated. Spoiler: your clients may not agree.

Next: Chapter 13 – Ignoring Compliance Because You're Not Regulated (Yet)

Chapter 13: Ignoring Compliance Because You're Not Regulated (Yet)

Introduction

Many small and mid-sized businesses assume compliance only matters if you're a hospital, a bank, or a Fortune 500 company. But in today's environment, **regulatory frameworks like SOC 2, GDPR, and HIPAA are showing up not just in laws — but in customer contracts, insurance questionnaires, and partnership requirements**. Compliance isn't just a legal checkbox anymore — it's a competitive baseline.

If you wait until you're legally required to comply, you may already be out of the running for key deals, clients, and renewals. In this chapter, we'll explain how compliance expectations are shifting, why SMBs can't afford to wait, and how to get ahead of the curve without getting buried in complexity.

Why Compliance Matters Before It's Mandatory

You don't have to be fined to feel the pain of non-compliance. Increasingly, **compliance is tied to trust** — and trust is tied to growth, especially in B2B relationships.

Compliance Is Becoming a Sales Requirement

Clients and partners are asking questions like:

- "Are you SOC 2 compliant?"
- "How do you protect customer data?"
- "Can you prove security controls?"

If you can't answer confidently — or if your competitors can — you're at a disadvantage, even if no one is legally forcing your hand.

Regulations Are Expanding Downstream

Bigger enterprises are being held accountable for their vendors. That means:

- If your customer is regulated, **you become part of their compliance risk**
- Insurance providers, investors, and partners now use compliance status as a **risk signal**

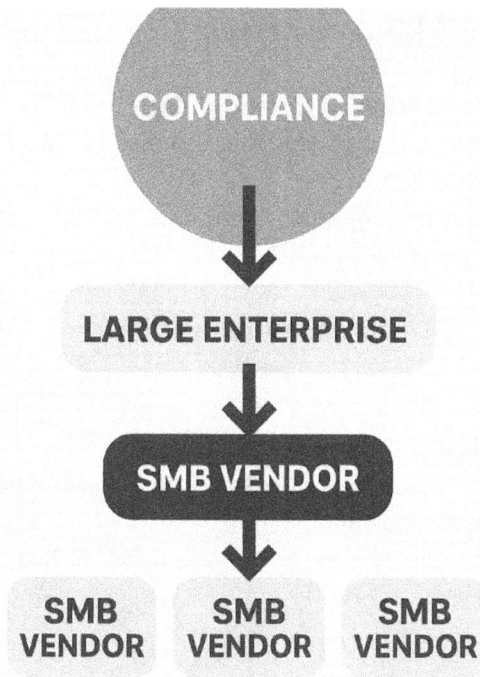

Demystifying the Big Frameworks

You've probably heard of these standards — but what do they mean for a small business?

SOC 2 (System and Organization Controls)

- Focus: **Data security, availability, processing integrity, confidentiality, and privacy**
- Applies to: Any business that stores or processes customer data (especially SaaS)
- Why it matters: Common requirement for B2B vendors; often part of due diligence

GDPR (General Data Protection Regulation)

- Focus: **Protection of personal data for EU citizens**
- Applies to: Any business that touches EU data — even if you're not in the EU
- Why it matters: Signals global data privacy maturity; impacts marketing, websites, CRMs

HIPAA (Health Insurance Portability and Accountability Act)

- Focus: **Health information security**
- Applies to: Healthcare orgs and **any vendor** handling protected health data
- Why it matters: Required if you serve the healthcare industry — directly or indirectly

COMPLIANCE	WHO	WHAT	WHY
SOC 2	Service providers storing customer data	Customer information	Ensures security controls
GDPR	Entities handling EU residents' data	Personal data	Protects privacy rights
HIPAA	Healthcare providers, plans, and clearinghouses	Heálthuard medical data	Safeguards medical data

What Happens When You Ignore Compliance

Even if regulators never knock on your door, ignoring compliance creates blind spots and lost business.

Common Scenarios

- A **prospective client walks away** because you can't answer their security questionnaire
- Your **cyber insurer denies coverage** or increases your premium
- You experience a **data breach** and lack the documentation to prove due diligence
- A partner **requires proof of compliance** — and you scramble to catch up

Tactical Best Practices for Getting Ahead

You don't need full certification to start meeting expectations. Here's how SMBs can build compliance readiness without overkill.

- Map your **data flows**: Understand what sensitive data you collect, store, and transmit
- Align with **a lightweight framework** (start with SOC 2 or CIS Controls)
- Maintain basic **security documentation** (policies, procedures, access logs)
- Build a **risk register** to track known issues or gaps
- Train staff on **data handling and privacy awareness**
- Practice **incident response** and document mock results

Common Pitfalls to Avoid

1. Waiting until it's urgent
Compliance readiness can't be rushed. Frameworks take time to implement, and shortcuts usually backfire under scrutiny.

2. Overengineering the solution
You don't need a 500-page binder. Most SMBs can meet early-stage compliance using simple, well-documented practices.

3. Treating compliance as IT-only
Leadership, HR, legal, and customer service all have roles to play. Compliance is cross-functional by nature.

4. Ignoring third-party risk
You're responsible for the security of your vendors — not just your own systems. This is often where audits start.

Real-World Example: Losing a Contract Over SOC 2

What Happened
A 20-person SaaS company in the HR tech space was shortlisted for a major enterprise contract. During procurement review, the client asked for SOC 2 documentation. The company had decent internal controls but no official audit or clear documentation.

What Went Wrong

- Couldn't produce clear access logs or policies
- Had no incident response plan or formal data retention policy
- Tried to "explain their controls" without structure

What We Learn

- Even without a breach, lack of documentation can kill a deal
- Preparing for compliance earns trust — especially with enterprise buyers
- Starting early gives you leverage when opportunity knocks

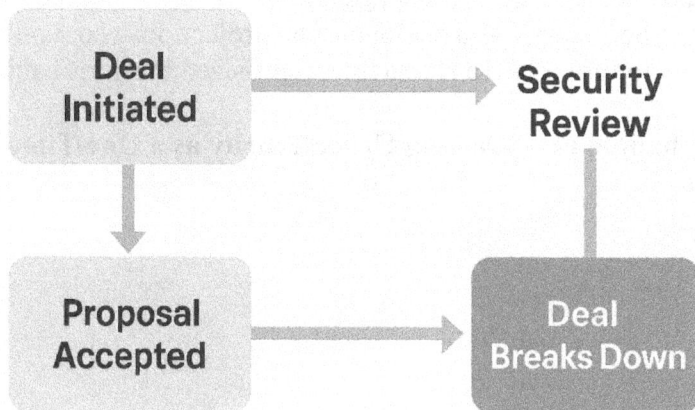

```
┌──────────────┐                    ┌──────────────┐
│    Deal      │ ─────────────────▶ │  Security    │
│  Initiated   │                    │  Review      │
└──────┬───────┘                    └──────────────┘
       │
       ▼
┌──────────────┐                    ┌──────────────┐
│  Proposal    │ ─────────────────▶ │    Deal      │
│  Accepted    │                    │ Breaks Down  │
└──────────────┘                    └──────────────┘
```

Compliance as a Trust Accelerator

Rather than viewing compliance as a chore, **use it as a business enabler**. It shows maturity, builds buyer confidence, and protects your team when something goes wrong.

A few simple, well-documented practices can elevate you above competitors and prepare you for future regulation — without hiring a compliance officer or buying expensive software.

Next Steps

Start by identifying what frameworks your industry or clients care about most. Run a self-assessment or work with a fractional CISO or MSP to map your current state. Document the basics: access policies, encryption practices, backup strategy, and incident response.

In the next chapter, we'll challenge another dangerous mindset — treating cybersecurity as a one-and-done project. Instead, you'll learn how to turn it into a repeatable, right-sized business habit.

Next: Chapter 14 – Treating Cybersecurity as a One-Time Project

Chapter 14: Treating Cybersecurity as a One-Time Project

Introduction

Too many businesses treat cybersecurity like an item on a to-do list — buy a firewall, check a box, move on. But cybersecurity isn't a one-and-done project. It's a living, evolving part of your business infrastructure, just like finance, HR, or operations. And if you're not updating your security posture regularly, you're falling behind — and exposing yourself to new threats by default.

In this chapter, we'll shift the mindset from reactive to proactive. You'll learn how to build lightweight, repeatable processes that scale with your business, and how to treat cybersecurity not as a single event, but as a continuous practice that protects your growth.

Why One-Time Thinking Fails

Security is not static. Threats evolve. Systems change. People make mistakes. A strategy that worked 12 months ago may be dangerously outdated today.

The Myth of "Set It and Forget It"

Too often, small and mid-sized businesses:

- Install tools without revisiting them
- Draft policies that go unread or unmaintained
- Launch one-time training events without reinforcement
- Perform security assessments, then file them away

Cybercriminals count on this inertia. They know your firewall is still using last year's rules — and that your team hasn't practiced a response since the last audit.

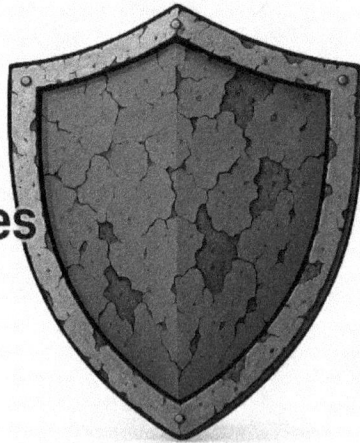

Security deteriorates over time

What Continuous Cybersecurity Looks Like

Moving from a project mindset to a process mindset doesn't mean overhauling your operations — it means building **security habits** into your existing rhythm.

Think in Cycles, Not Events

Strong cybersecurity includes regular, manageable activities like:

- **Quarterly risk reviews** (What's changed? What's exposed?)
- **Ongoing patch management** (Are we up to date?)
- **Monthly access reviews** (Who has access to what — and should they?)
- **Annual tabletop exercises** (How would we respond to an incident today?)

Lightweight, Repeatable Routines

You don't need a dedicated security team to stay secure. You need repeatable processes that:

- Can be owned by non-technical leaders
- Fit into existing team meetings or operations reviews
- Have clear documentation and accountability

LIGHTWEIGHT CYBERSECURITY CYCLES

	JANUARY	FEBRUARY	MARCH	APRIL
QUARTERLY				
MONTHLY				
ANNUAL				

Tactical Process Examples for SMBs

1. Quarterly Security Snapshot
A short leadership meeting reviewing:

- New systems or vendors added
- Any incidents, phishing attempts, or vulnerabilities
- Status of backup tests and patching

2. Access Review Checklist (Monthly)

- Review staff list: Who's joined, left, or changed roles?
- Remove stale admin accounts or unnecessary permissions
- Verify MFA is enabled across the board

3. Annual Response Drill
Pick a realistic scenario (ransomware, insider breach, lost laptop) and run a tabletop:

- What's the first step?
- Who communicates with whom?
- Can we restore data quickly?
- What logs or documentation would we need?

Common Pitfalls to Avoid

1. Treating cybersecurity like a task for "IT"
Leadership, HR, finance, and operations all have a role. Security is a business-wide responsibility, not a technical silo.

2. Relying on tools without process
A security product without an active process is like a fire alarm no one checks. Tools are only effective when configured, monitored, and reviewed.

3. Skipping reviews because "nothing happened"
No news doesn't mean no risk. Quiet periods are the best time to spot small issues before they explode.

4. Confusing compliance with security
You can pass an audit and still be vulnerable. Compliance is a snapshot. Cybersecurity is a movie.

Real-World Example: The Forgotten Firewall

What Happened
A growing logistics company installed a business-grade firewall when they moved into a new office. But three years later, they suffered a breach — and discovered the firmware hadn't been updated once since installation.

What Went Wrong

- No one owned firewall maintenance
- Security wasn't included in quarterly ops reviews
- Logs were never enabled — they had no idea when the breach occurred

What We Learn

- Security controls must be managed continuously
- Assign ownership — someone must be responsible for maintenance
- Integrate cybersecurity into routine operational check-ins

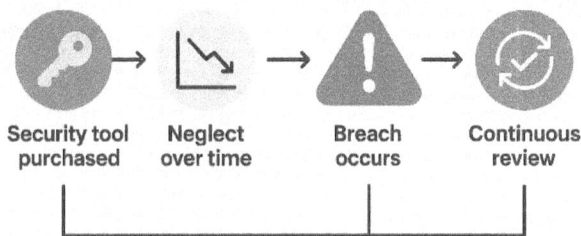

Security tool purchased → Neglect over time → Breach occurs → Continuous review

Actionable Framework: Cybersecurity as a Business Habit

Here's a simple way to bake cybersecurity into the rhythm of your company:

Frequency	Activity	Owner
Monthly	Access review	HR or Ops
Quarterly	Risk and patch review	IT/MSP
Bi-Annually	Phishing test and retraining	IT + Team Leads
Annually	Tabletop incident response drill	Leadership + IT

Don't overcomplicate it. Build **just enough structure to keep the conversation alive** — and let the process evolve with your business.

Conclusion

Cybersecurity isn't a product you buy — it's a muscle you build. Businesses that treat it as a one-time project leave themselves exposed to growing threats and shrinking trust. But those who integrate it as a habit gain resilience, customer confidence, and peace of mind.

Next Steps

Start small. Choose one activity — maybe a monthly access review — and make it part of your normal ops. From there, add quarterly and annual practices. As you build momentum, your business will become more secure without feeling the burden.

In the next chapter, we'll explore the financial side of preparedness — why failing to calculate the true cost of downtime can derail everything you've built.

Next: Chapter 15 – Failing to Calculate the Real Cost of Downtime

Chapter 15: Failing to Calculate the Real Cost of Downtime

Introduction

When businesses think about cyber risk, they often focus on data — protecting it, encrypting it, recovering it. But **data loss isn't the only or even the most immediate cost of a cyberattack.** What hits hardest is downtime. When your systems go offline, your business stops earning, your customers get frustrated, and your reputation takes a hit that money can't always fix.

Despite this, many small and mid-sized businesses (SMBs) have no idea what an hour of downtime actually costs them — let alone a day or a week. In this final chapter, we'll break down how to calculate the true cost of being offline, identify critical systems, and make smarter investments in resilience before disaster strikes.

Downtime: The Hidden Business Killer

Downtime is more than an IT problem — it's a **business interruption**. And its impact compounds quickly across people, processes, and reputation.

Where the Real Costs Show Up

- **Lost revenue** from missed transactions or delayed operations
- **Employee productivity** frozen while systems are unavailable
- **Customer trust** eroded due to missed deadlines, lack of communication, or service disruption
- **Brand damage** amplified by social media, news coverage, or client churn
- **Regulatory penalties** from failing to meet data availability or breach notification requirements

LAYERS OF DOWNTIME COST

DIRECT
Revenue

INDIRECT
Productivity

LONG-TERM
Reputation

Even Short Outages Hurt

For many SMBs, even one hour of downtime can disrupt cash flow or delivery timelines. If it happens during a peak time — tax season, holiday sales, contract closing — the effects can be devastating.

How to Calculate Your Real Downtime Cost

Understanding your risk starts with measuring what's at stake. Here's a simple formula for estimating the financial cost of downtime:

Downtime Cost = (Revenue Loss + Productivity Loss + Recovery Cost + Intangible Impacts)

Break it down:

- **Revenue Loss**
  Estimate your average revenue per hour/day, and how much business halts when systems go offline.
- **Productivity Loss**
  How many employees are impacted? Multiply their hourly cost by downtime hours.
- **Recovery Cost**
  Include costs like emergency IT labor, incident response vendors, and rush logistics.
- **Intangible Impacts**
  These are harder to quantify but crucial — client trust, reputation, long-term customer retention.

DOWNTIME COST CALCULATOR

Hourly Revenue	$2,500
Number of Employees	20
Hourly Recovery Cost	$300
Estimated Downtime	4 hours

CALCULATE

Identify Your Critical Systems

Not every system has the same impact when it fails. To prepare effectively, you need to know which platforms and tools are **mission-critical.**

Ask These Questions:

- What systems do we need to **make money**?
- What do our customers rely on to **get service**?
- What systems hold or process **sensitive or regulated data**?
- If this system went offline for a day, **what would stop working**?

Examples of critical systems for SMBs:

- E-commerce platforms and payment processors
- CRM and sales systems
- Email and internal communication platforms
- Line-of-business software (accounting, inventory, dispatch)
- Cloud drives or file storage systems

Tactical Best Practices to Minimize Downtime Risk

You don't need enterprise budgets to reduce downtime risk. Just smart prioritization and proactive planning.

- Identify and regularly **test backups** of all critical systems
- Document **manual fallback procedures** (e.g., phone orders if e-commerce is down)
- Build **redundancy** for high-risk systems (cloud replication, secondary internet connection)
- Monitor uptime and **log incidents** to learn from small outages
- Maintain a **vendor contact sheet** for fast support escalation
- Review cyber insurance to ensure **business interruption coverage** is adequate

Common Pitfalls to Avoid

1. Underestimating impact due to partial outages
You may still "have internet," but if your order processing or customer support is down, you're losing money and trust.

2. Believing you're "too small" to need a recovery plan

Attackers target SMBs specifically because they often lack resilience. Your size makes planning even more essential — not less.

3. Assuming cloud equals uptime

Cloud systems can still go down — and when they do, your fallback plan matters. Always understand your provider's SLAs and responsibilities.

4. Delaying until after a close call

Don't wait for a minor outage to show you where you're vulnerable. Use that warning to act now.

Real-World Example: One Day, $80K Gone

What Happened

A regional construction company relied on a cloud-based project management system to coordinate teams, access blueprints, and submit invoices. When a misconfigured update caused their platform to crash on a Monday morning, the entire operation stalled.

What Went Wrong

- No documented manual process for field teams
- No local copies of project files
- No clear point of contact at the vendor for urgent support
- Teams waited instead of switching to alternate workflows

Result

Subcontractors were idled, client deadlines were missed, and the company had to pay overtime to catch up. Estimated loss: $80,000 in one business day.

What We Learn

- Downtime is real money — even in non-digital industries
- Vendor risk is business risk
- Local contingencies and rapid communication can dramatically reduce impact

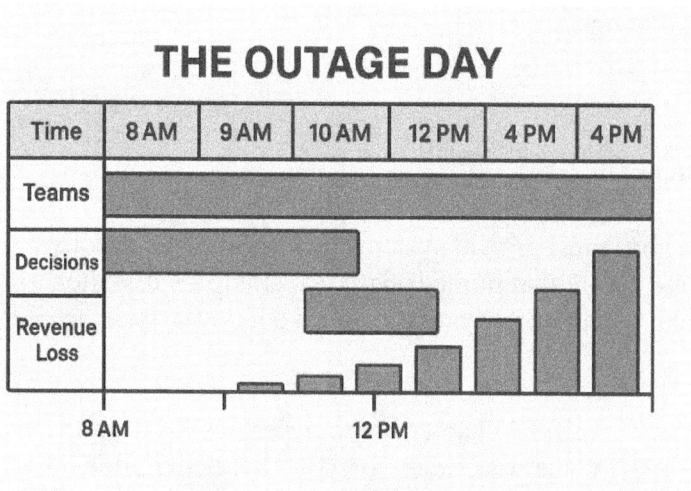

THE OUTAGE DAY

Time	8 AM	9 AM	10 AM	12 PM	4 PM	4 PM
Teams						
Decisions						
Revenue Loss						

8 AM   12 PM

Simple Downtime Readiness Checklist

Use this checklist to quickly assess your preparedness:

- ☑ We've calculated estimated cost of 1 hour and 1 day of downtime
- ☑ We've identified and documented our most critical systems
- ☑ We have tested recovery steps for each key system
- ☑ We know our vendor SLAs and have escalation contacts
- ☑ We've rehearsed what to do during a system outage
- ☑ Our insurance policy includes business interruption coverage

Conclusion

Downtime isn't just an inconvenience — it's a direct threat to your bottom line, customer trust, and business continuity. By measuring what's at stake and preparing accordingly, you move from reactive to resilient. Cybersecurity isn't just about defense — it's about recovery. And recovery is what keeps your business alive when things go wrong.

Next Steps

Review your most critical systems and estimate your hourly cost of downtime. Share that number with leadership — it's often a wake-up call. Then identify one system to build a recovery plan around this month.

While this is the final chapter in the series, it's far from the end of your journey. Cyber risk doesn't rest — but neither does your ability to prepare, adapt, and grow stronger with every decision.

Stay vigilant. Stay practical. And keep security aligned with the business you're building.

CHECK YOUR BONUS AT THE END !

Glossary of Key Terms

Covering All 15 Chapters – SMB Cybersecurity Fundamentals

This glossary defines critical terms used throughout the 15 chapters. Each entry is written for **non-technical business leaders**, providing clear, actionable understanding without jargon.

A

Access Review
A regular audit of who has access to systems, files, and tools — ensuring employees only have the permissions they need and nothing more.

Air-Gapped Backup
A backup stored offline or on a system not connected to your production network. Used to prevent ransomware from encrypting backups along with active files.

Attack Surface
The total number of ways an attacker could try to access your systems or data. The more tools, logins, and connections you have, the larger the surface.

B

Backup (Data Backup)
A secure, restorable copy of your business data. Backups are critical for recovering from cyberattacks, hardware failures, and accidental deletion.

Business Continuity
The ability of your business to keep operating during and after a disruption, like a cyberattack or system failure.

Business Interruption Insurance
A type of coverage that compensates you for lost income during downtime caused by events like cyberattacks or disasters.

C

Cloud Backup
Data backups stored in offsite cloud infrastructure (like AWS, Azure, Google Cloud). Provides geographic redundancy and faster disaster recovery.

Compliance
The act of meeting legal or industry-specific requirements for security, privacy, and data protection (e.g., SOC 2, HIPAA, GDPR).

Critical Systems
The systems, applications, or platforms your business relies on to generate revenue, communicate, or deliver products/services.

Cyber Hygiene
Ongoing best practices to reduce security risk — like updating software, enabling MFA, and regularly reviewing access controls.

D

Data Breach
Unauthorized access, use, or disclosure of sensitive or protected information — often leading to legal and reputational consequences.

Data Loss
When data is permanently destroyed, deleted, or becomes inaccessible due to cyber incidents, errors, or hardware failure.

Disaster Recovery
The process of restoring systems and data after a major disruption — often tied to having backups and a documented plan.

Downtime
Any period during which systems or services are unavailable — often leading to productivity loss, missed revenue, or customer dissatisfaction.

E

Endpoint
Any device that connects to your business network (laptops, desktops, phones, etc.) — often a common target for attacks.

Encryption
A method of scrambling data so that it's unreadable without a secret key — critical for protecting files, backups, and communications.

F

Firewall
A network security tool that filters incoming and outgoing traffic based on security rules — acts like a gatekeeper for your business network.

G

GDPR (General Data Protection Regulation)
European Union regulation requiring strong data privacy and protection for any business handling EU personal data, even if based outside Europe.

H

HIPAA (Health Insurance Portability and Accountability Act)
A U.S. regulation governing the security and privacy of health information — critical for any company handling medical data.

I

Incident
Any event that compromises the confidentiality, integrity, or availability of business systems or data. Not all incidents are breaches, but all require action.

Incident Response Plan (IRP)
A documented guide that outlines how your team should detect, contain, communicate, and recover from cyber incidents.

Insider Threat
Risks that come from employees or contractors — either maliciously or accidentally — who expose or compromise company data.

L

Least Privilege
A principle where users only have access to the data and systems necessary for their role — reduces the impact of stolen or misused accounts.

M

Malware
Malicious software designed to damage or compromise systems — includes ransomware, viruses, keyloggers, and spyware.

Multi-Factor Authentication (MFA)
A security method that requires users to verify their identity with **two or more factors** (e.g., password + code sent to phone).

O

Offline Backup
A data copy that's stored in a location not connected to the internet or your active systems — resistant to ransomware and network failures.

P

Patch Management
The routine process of updating software to fix known vulnerabilities and improve security.

Phishing

A type of cyberattack where attackers trick users into giving up sensitive information or clicking malicious links — often disguised as legitimate emails or texts.

Playbook (Security)

A simplified, step-by-step guide your team follows during an incident or key security process — especially useful in high-pressure moments.

Productivity Loss

Revenue or efficiency lost when employees can't do their jobs during a system outage or incident.

R

Ransomware

A type of malware that locks or encrypts your data until a ransom is paid — often targeting SMBs with weak defenses or untested backups.

Recovery Point Objective (RPO)

The maximum amount of data you can afford to lose, measured in time. For example, if your RPO is 4 hours, backups must run at least that often.

Recovery Time Objective (RTO)

How fast you need systems back online after an incident. Defines the acceptable downtime before the business is seriously impacted.

Resilience (Cyber Resilience)

Your business's ability to anticipate, withstand, recover from, and adapt to cyber threats or disruptions.

Risk Register

A living document that lists your cybersecurity risks, potential impacts, and mitigation efforts — a core tool in governance and compliance.

S

SaaS (Software-as-a-Service)
Cloud-based applications accessed via the internet (like Microsoft 365, QuickBooks Online). Often require separate backup and security considerations.

Security Questionnaire
A set of compliance and risk questions your company may need to answer to win contracts or prove cybersecurity maturity to partners.

Security Training
Ongoing education for employees to recognize threats, use systems safely, and reduce the risk of human error or social engineering attacks.

SLA (Service Level Agreement)
A contract that defines uptime, support response, and recovery expectations with technology providers or MSPs.

SOC 2 (System and Organization Controls)
A framework for demonstrating secure data handling and operations — commonly requested by clients in B2B SaaS and tech.

T

Tabletop Exercise
A rehearsal of how your team would respond to a cyber incident — walking through roles, decisions, and response steps without real impact.

Third-Party Risk
Security or compliance vulnerabilities that arise from your vendors or service providers — especially those who store or process your data.

U

Uptime
The percentage of time your systems are available and functional. High uptime = strong service continuity.

V

Vendor Risk Management
The process of assessing and managing the cybersecurity posture of third-party providers — critical when outsourcing IT, cloud storage, or business apps.

Vulnerability
A weakness in your system, software, or processes that could be exploited by a threat actor.

W

Workflow Recovery Plan
A manual or alternate process your team follows to continue operating when systems are down — essential to minimize disruption during downtime.

This glossary is your reference toolkit — designed to clarify, not confuse. Bookmark it, print it, or share it with your leadership team. **Clear understanding leads to better decision-making — and better protection.**

Bonus – FREE eBook Version

Want the full-color PDF version of this book?
Simply email me at **ericl@acrasolution.com** with a **screenshot of your Amazon purchase and positive review**, and I'll gladly send you your personal copy.

Thank you for taking the time to read this eBook.

Your support means more than you know. **By purchasing this book, you're directly contributing to the creation of more high-quality, practical resources** for business owners, IT leaders, and everyday professionals navigating the complex world of cybersecurity. It's because of readers like you that I can continue researching, writing, and delivering tools that make a real difference.

Whether you leave a positive review, recommend this book to a colleague, or simply apply what you've learned — **you're helping grow a stronger, safer business community. And for that, I sincerely thank you.**

At **AcraSolution**, we're committed to providing both premium services and a wide range of **free, actionable tools**. Our growing library includes documentation, articles, and step-by-step guides — designed to bring you immediate value, no strings attached.

If you need additional guidance or support, don't hesitate to visit our website www.acrasolution.com or reach out directly.

Together, we can build a more secure future.

— Eric LeBouthillier
Author & Cybersecurity Strategist

www.ingramcontent.com/pod-product-compliance
Lightning Source LLC
Chambersburg PA
CBHW071716210326
41597CB00017B/2504